A WISE APPLE TREE HELPS ME...

TOP TIPS FOR WISE KIDS

By Andrew Holt

A Wise Apple Tree Helps Me; top tips for wise kids
© Andrew Holt 2015

National Library of Australia Cataloguing-in-Publication entry

Creator:	Holt, Andrew, 1973- author.
Title:	A wise apple tree helps me...: top tips for wise kids / Andrew Holt.
ISBN:	9780994336316 (paperback)
Target Audience:	For primary school age.
Subjects:	Self-esteem--Juvenile literature. Mindfulness (Psychology)--Juvenile literature. Positive psychology--Juvenile literature.
Dewey Number:	158.1

Published by Andrew Holt
Design and layout by Sassy Branding
www.sassybranding.com
Printed by InHouse Publishing
www.inhousepublishing.com.au

Andrew Holt

Andrew Holt writes books for children of all ages. A primary school teacher, yoga teacher, acting principal, and mindfulness trainer, Andrew has travelled the world working with parents and children from many different cultures. With a kid's sense of adventure he's explored the deserts of Australia, the dark jungles of Indonesia, the ancient Himalayan mountains of India and Nepal, and the rolling grasslands of Africa.

Andrew's experiences have brought him to the conclusion that wisdom isn't just for old folks. Kids have their own valuable perspectives on the world too—if we only listen to them. So it is Andrew's mission to open the world for these wise kids, and have as much fun as he can while doing so.

His first book, *A Wise Apple Tree Helps Me: Top Tips for Wise Kids*, was released in September 2015.

You can find out more on his Facebook author page, Andrew Holt.

Introduction

In 2008 I had one of those 'aha' moments in teaching. Most teachers face the constant dilemma of listening to and 'sorting' through students who have had some sort of conflict during their lunchtime breaks. It was one such day that I looked to the heavens and cried in humorous exasperation, "I just want someone to tell me a good story ... does anybody have a good news story to tell?"

It was in that moment that I realised where my attention/energy was going. Kids love attention, either good or bad, so long as it is attention. I suddenly realised in that moment that I was focusing and modelling MY attention to areas of conflict and conflict resolution. One part of me argued that I, with good intentions, was listening to each side of the stories of conflict or complaint, and using various strategies to get students to resolve the 'problem', often by asking them, "What could you do differently next time?" But I realised that the root cause was that they/we/I were focusing on the problems and the negatives!!! Most of our attention went to the problem! Where attention goes, so does energy grow.

So we got together as a class and discussed what we wanted to see in the playground. The first things that most of the students started telling me were: no teasing, no bullying, no this, no that, etc. I was a little shocked as no-one was telling me what they DID want to see. We then listed what we wanted to to see, say, hear, feel, and do. These included such things as kindness, helpfulness, friendliness, etc.

These observations, along with learning more about the mind and brain, as well as reflecting on my life and drawing from my teaching experience, were the motivation behind creating and sharing this book. *A Wise Apple Tree Helps Me: Top Tips for Wise Kids* is a rhyming book for kids of all ages.

This book contains research drawn from both modern and ancient wisdoms and psychology, presented in simple rhymes. While these truths are nothing new to most, my intention for every reader is to increase their awareness, and for them to remind themselves how to be their best selves and consciously learn to focus on what they want to be, do, and have.

It is so important to be the change we wish to see in the world and in the children we have in our care. The language and actions we model are so influential in setting up the foundations of our children's being. This is often so hard to do when our buttons are being pushed. The rhymes in *A Wise Apple Tree Helps Me: Top Tips for Wise Kids* are important reminders, not only for our children, but for us adults too.

This book also fits perfectly within the Australian Curriculum under the 'General Capabilities' banner relating to the 'The Personal and Social Capability Learning

Continuum'. This section organises itself into the four interrelated areas of self-awareness, self-management, social awareness, and social management. Each of these elements are themes throughout this book.

A Wise Apple Tree Helps Me: Top Tips for Wise Kids has been set out in chapters to read separately, or it can be read from the start to the finish. Enjoy reading this book with your children, discussing the many concepts it contains, and how these can be integrated into your life.

Both the stand alone children's book and the accompanied colouring book complement each other. The accompanied colouring/exercise book allows for reflection and deeper integration into the brain of the many concepts within.

Space is included after each chapter, where the reader can share their own personal responses using their own wisdoms, insights, rhymes, or illustrations that have come from personal experience. This new awareness and these shifts in thinking can come about as results of possible discussions whilst reading the book with peers, family members, teachers, or therapists.

I thank the many people, including all the children I have ever taught and learnt from, to colleagues, family, and friends, and all who I have met on this amazing book/ life journey. Our everyday thoughts, words, speech, responses, and actions have contributed in some way to what is present in this book today.

May you find peaceful, happy, loving thoughts, in creating the reality you wish to call the 'present', knowing that these thoughts and actions create a new page in the chapter of your life's journey, right now, today!

"If you focus on the bad,

you'll be mad or sad,

so focus on what's alright,

and you'll be a bright shining light."

Much Gratitude

Andrew Holt

Testimonials

"It is a unique book that will be very helpful. It has very good meanings and will sell out!"
- Solomon McDonald, age eleven, Grade 5

"Andrew's commitment and dedication to taking his message beyond the classroom is commendable. What I love about this book and the message Andrew is sharing, is the simplicity of mindfulness. If we can teach our kids at an early age to embrace this way of thinking and being, the world will be a much better place. Read it to your kids, get them thinking differently, and be the change we need to see. It's been a delight to design and typeset this book Andrew, your illustrations are fabulous!"
- Jeanne Treloar, Sassy Branding

"I believe Andrew has successfully captured many of the everyday challenges in the life of a child. It is great to read a book that provides strategies to empower a child to think positively even when faced with challenging situations. The voice of Grandpa Joe as a mentor for Sam promotes respect for elders and emphasises the importance of family support. There is no greater gift we can bestow upon a child than a feeling of self-worth, and this book certainly assists in empowering children to trust their values and beliefs."
- Pam Erfurt, Principal, Moil Primary School, Moil, Northern Territory, Australia

"This book inspired me to make my own rhyme: 'If you focus on the good, then you will do what you should."
- Crystal Holmes, age twelve, Grade 6

"Andrew is a wealth of knowledge when it comes to educating and caring for our younger generation. He is able to teach a range of tools and techniques in order to empower kids, teenagers, and adults. With experience gained over many years of teaching and travelling around the world, he entertains and engages an audience through rhyme and storytelling. Andrew has the ability to impart important messages, while also sharing his sense of fun and adventure. This is an inspirational book that will assist many as they go through the ups and downs of life. Kids will be asking for more!"
- Brenda Carige B.Ed, Dip.T.

"Thank you for sharing your gorgeous book with my daughter and myself, we thoroughly enjoyed it. We really loved reading this together, my daughter loved the rhyming and I loved how each chapter discussed a different topic. It was like a key we could use to open a door of discussion on so many topics that perhaps aren't always talked about in daily life. Great format, loved the pictures, and it kept the attention of my nine-year-old."
- Samantha Allimant, mother of a nine-year-old

"This book has the best tips for kids than most other books have."
- Imogen Stride, age twelve, Grade 6

"Every time I read this book I feel overwhelmed with joy and gratitude, not only for the consciousness it embodies but for the fact that there are teachers out there who 'get it' and who are leading our children along with us on a more mindful, enlightened journey. One of the best children's books I have ever read. Well done Andrew."
- Sam Morley, mother of three.

Wise Kids - Which tips are for you?

Asking for Help

"Grandpa Joe, at school you see,
there's lots of people picking on me.
I don't know what to think, say, or do and
I've had enough,
I want to quit, it's far too tough."

"Even at home I feel like I'm in a bubble,
because I make mistakes and get into trouble.
I don't know what to think, say, or do,
so I just go hide and sit on the loo!"

Grandpa Joe then said ...

"Young Sam, there are some things I believe
you should know,
a few little tips that will help you grow,
so be sure to listen, my dear grandson,
as this can change your sadness to fun ..."

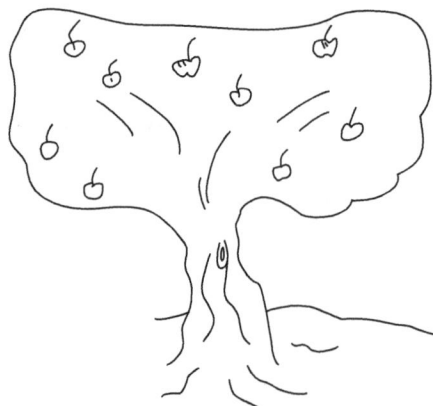

Who do you ask for help?

school

Hi Sam, you're looking worried. What's up?

Hi Grandpa Joe

home

I have courage to ask for help to help me grow.

Train your Brain

"Let's sit under this wise old apple tree,
many stories it has witnessed under thee.
So we can simply be still and discover the key,
to grow happiness in you, and be free."

"It starts, young Sam, with the most important
thing to train,
it's not eating, it's not a sport, nor even flying to Spain.
That number one thing you need to train,
is watching those thoughts and words that visit
your brain."

"For your thoughts are where it all begins,
being aware of them helps your successful wins."

How will you train your brain?

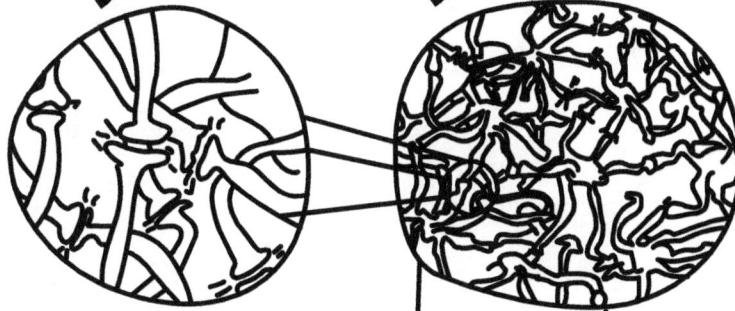

I can see it's up to me to train my mind.

SELF TALK - Fertiliser and Poisionous

*"Young Sam, become your own computer engineer,
as you see those thoughts that you want to appear."*

"Where is your thinking, young one,
When you make a mistake in front of everyone?
Do you poison yourself and say,
I'm dumb, useless, I hate myself today?"

"Or do you fertilise yourself and say: 'I'll be alright,
I promise myself not to get mad and uptight.
I'll tell myself I will get it, I know I will,
Because my mind is my magic pill.' "

"Being aware of your self-talk, can help you think.
It programs your mind to create a strong neural link.
So, my grandson, do your best to focus on
what you want to think,
and just watch and let float by those
thoughts that stink."

'How can I program my brain today?"

"By choosing the words you want to say and hear each day. This is your fertiliser"

Fertiliser Thinking   Poisonous Thinking

OR

I choose to think strong.

Focus on What's Alright

"If you focus on the bad,
you'll be mad or sad,
so focus on what's alright,
and you'll be a bright shining light."

"You're a detective who focuses on each clue,
so, grandson, what happens next is up to you!
Learn your responses, they are the key,
in deciding how your journey will be."

'Grandpa Joe, everything is bad at school and home!"

"Sam, yes that may be true. But can you find one thing that has been alright in your life today?"

What's alright?

I focus on what's alright.

Kind Acts

"Sam, you'll see, practicing kindness with
yourself and others,
will surely help all your friends, sisters, and brothers.
Being aware of what you do and say,
can also help someone have a great day."

"Share these lessons with kind acts of joy,
a song, some flowers, your smile, a toy!
Using this helps in your mind's training,
do something now, everyone is gaining."

What kind acts will you do today?

Action Creates a Chain Reaction

**"Focus on what action you want to do,
and send the rest to the zoo."**

"Plan, focus, believe, and do,
taking these steps is up to you.
And as you act, you'll progress,
so do your best to achieve success."

"Remember, Sam, your action is required,
to get the results that are desired.
What you give out helps to create,
a ripple effect beyond this date."

What ripple effect are you creating?

What could happen next?

One, two, three, it's up to ME!

My Style is

"Others can say things that hurt,
which can stick like pieces of dirt.
Ask yourself, 'Is it true?'
If it's not … let it unglue."

"But if there's a little truth to what they say,
can you think of a better way?
Change your thinking to what feels better,
rewrite your hero's journey in a new style of letter."

"Grandpa, What is a hero's journey?"

"Its your life you write each day through facing the challenges that come your way?"

What Style will you choose?

AGRO
(mad and mean)

WEAK
(sad and hurt)

COOL AND CONFIDENT

Thinking of a Better Way

I choose my style to be cool and friendly.

The Present

**"Sam, be here, look at this apple right now—
and watch out for your wandering cow!"**

"My grandson, the past is gone,
let it go and move on.
The future is yet to appear—
why worry about what's not here."

"Now is a present for you to enjoy,
unwrap this gift, and yell, 'Ahoy!'
This moment is here for you to shine
in sharing strengths by your design!"

"What do you mean by my wandering cow, Grandpa?"

"It's my mind isn't it?"

"What do you think it means Sam?

Yes! That's what I meant, Sam. How wise you are"

Watch out! Stay focused!

I am here to shine NOW!

Be Still

"Sam, to slow your wandering mind's chatter,
focus on the things that really matter."

"Use your breath to quieten and hush,
learn to just watch, be patient, don't rush,
in and out, slowly through the nose,
imagine the air going down to your toes."

"When worried and muddled in your head,
use legs and feet on the earth instead.
Imagine this apple tree is you, strong and still,
sending roots deep with all your will."

How can I calm my mind?

Breathe deeply 1,2,3,4 pushing my belly out like a balloon.

Slowly

Breatheback 1,2,3,4, releasing the air.

Squeeze your muscles, then let go and be still

In and out through the nose.

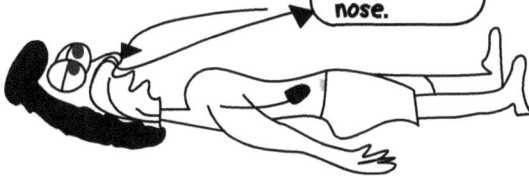

When worried try...

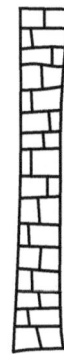

I can choose to still my body and feel calm.

Gratitude

**"Sam, another tip for you
to help you to stop feeling blue:
focus on being grateful in your life today,
as this sows seeds of happiness forever-and-a-day."**

Be thankful for this EARTH that SUPPORTS YOU.
She GIVES and GIVES so much that is new.
Think of all the things you get,
and all your needs that are met.

From where do they come?
It's the EARTH that is your MUM.
She shares so much that is a TREAT—
wood, metal, rock, trees, and meat.
Lakes, rivers, mountains too,
veggies, fruit, and crops she grew.

"I'm grateful for . . ."

"Sam can you name five things that you are grateful for today?"

What are you grateful for?

"Through gratitude and working together with the Earth and each other as a team, we can create incredible masterpieces, Sam'

I am grateful for all I have now.

My Masterpiece Will Be...

"You too, Sam, are like this earth that turns and flows,
deciding what you will make, that either burns or grows.
How will you use your tools to create
your own masterpiece from love or hate?"

"Remember that you and the earth are the same,
both need to be treated with kindness and respect,
not shame.
Giving thanks to yourself and others goes a long way,
in sharing happiness each and every day."

"Yes, I love the shade
the tree gives us right
now too!"

"Look, smell, feel and
taste this beautiful
apple. What a natural
masterpiece this tree
has grown!"

truth

helpful

friendly

kindness

happy

I CHOOSE ...

mean

nasty

lying

teasing

Love

Hate

THANKS LIST

- mum
- dad
- food
- school
- house
- healthy body
- toys
- trees
- water
- garden / park / swimming pool

- grandparents
- family
- friends
- pets
- bed

- teacher
- beach
- clothes

Put in Rubbish in the Bin

BE PEACEFUL

Look after my land & water

Take care of the animals

Take care of rivers

Share my gifts!

I take care of Mother Earth.

Plan Your Success

"Set a **goal** for each day,
to help you grow, learn, and play."
Create a **vision board** to help set you free,
For the things you want to have, feel, and see."

"Draw, write, cut and paste
your vision without any haste!
Put this poster on a wall,
to help you grow so strong and tall."

"Look at your vision board each day,
close your eyes and **see** it at play.
Feel, **believe**, and **know** it is real,
so clap your hands like a happy seal."

"I plan to come here each day to relax and eat mindfully."

"What's mindfully?"

"It means focusing on what is happening in the now moment."

Have you made a plan?

I plan for my dreams to come true.

What Does My Body Need?

"Grandson, focus on feeling what your body needs,
as this is the only one you have to succeed.
Is your body saying 'I need a drink,' or, 'Take a rest'?
Or do you get up and move to be your best?
Can you feel when your body wants to stop and say,
it's not safe or healthy for you to do this today?"

"The seasons gives clues, deciding, more or less,
supporting your body in how to eat, play, and dress."

"I'm here for your weekly massage Grandpa Joe?"

"Thanks Catherine. My body needs it."

"My body feels like playing on the swings, Grandpa?"

"O.k, be safe. I'm not far away."

Does my body need *more* or *less* of these to keep me strong?

Be safe, exercise, sleep, water,
healthy food, exercise and fun

I know what my body needs to be strong.

Relax to Achieve Your Max

"It's important to RELAX each day,
and to let any worries pass away.
You can use music to chill and be still,
paint, draw, do exercises—whatever your will."

"Take a break from what you do,
drinking water will help you too.
Being in nature will help you be calm,
'relaxed' will then be part of your charm."

How do you relax?

I take a break and relax each day.

Fears

**"Sam, if something does not work out as you have planned,
face your fears with courage … take a stand."**

"As this is part of your journey, be ready,
to use your hero strengths to climb back up and be steady.
This may mean you take a different way,
to reach the goal you dreamt of today."

"Are you O.K? You might need to try a different way?"

Which apple will you bite today?

Courage

Kindness

Humour

Teamwork

Helpfulness

Resilience

Friendly

Personal Best

Organised

Persistence

Compassion

Trust

Leadership

Honesty

Patience

Forgiveness

I can handle any situation by using my hero strengths.

Wise Apple Tree and Me

"Sam, from our talks today, did you understand that
YOU are the KEY?
That can solve either the sadness, madness, or
happiness mystery?
Your choices and responses are always the key,
in learning how you want to be."

"Sam, remember when you see this beautiful red apple
tree,
that it is similar to both you and me."

Then Sam replied, and said ...

"Wow, thanks! I feel so much better, Grandpa Joe,
with all these wise tips to practice and sow.
Until I see you next time, here is my high-five touch!
So take care, because I love you so much."

How is the Apple Tree similar to you and me?

I am strong like this wise apple tree.

Some similar ways, can you think of others?

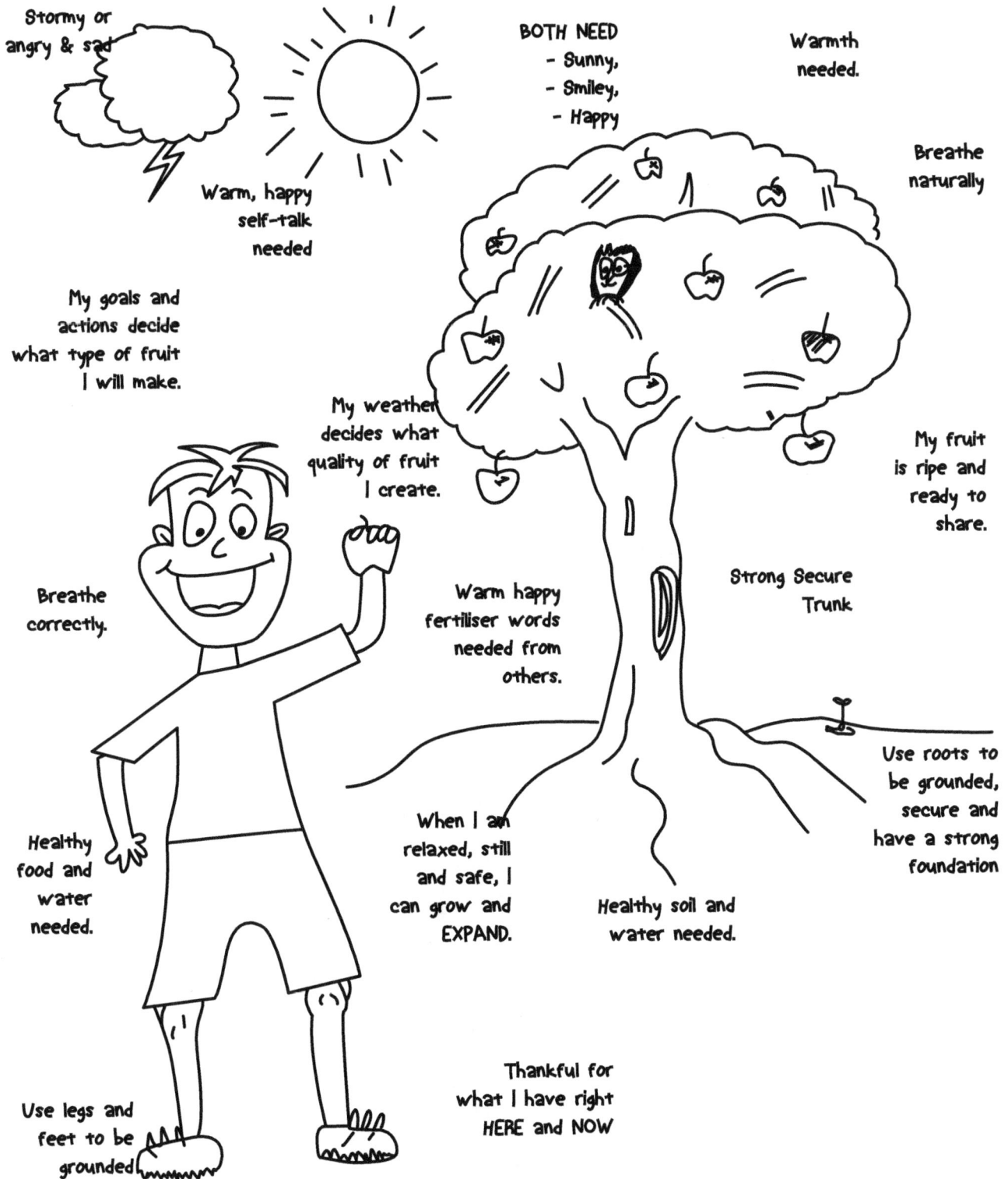

Stormy or angry & sad

BOTH NEED
- Sunny,
- Smiley,
- Happy

Warmth needed.

Warm, happy self-talk needed

Breathe naturally

My goals and actions decide what type of fruit I will make.

My weather decides what quality of fruit I create.

My fruit is ripe and ready to share.

Breathe correctly.

Strong Secure Trunk

Warm happy fertiliser words needed from others.

Use roots to be grounded, secure and have a strong foundation

Healthy food and water needed.

When I am relaxed, still and safe, I can grow and EXPAND.

Healthy soil and water needed.

Use legs and feet to be grounded

Thankful for what I have right HERE and NOW

I am strong like this wise apple tree.

This book is dedicated to the benefit of all beings. It is written with devotion and unconditional love and gratitude to all wise teachers, masters, saints, and sages of both past and present. May they and their teachings and wisdom continue to awaken, within every individual, the light of who they really are.